THE CROONING WIND

Three Greenlandic Poets

THE CROONING WIND

Three Greenlandic Poets

Torkilk Mørch

Gerda Hvisterdahl

Innunquaq Larsen

translated by

Nive Grønkjær and David R. Slavitt

newamericanpress

Milwaukee, Wisconsin • *Urbana, Illinois*

newamericanpress

www.NewAmericanPress.com

© 2012 by David R. Slavitt

Printed in the United States of America

ISBN 978-0-9849439-3-7

For ordering information, please contact:

Ingram Book Group
One Ingram Blvd.
La Vergne, TN 37086
(800) 937-8000
orders@ingrambook.com

CONTENTS

Gerda Hvisterdahl

Innunquaq Larsen

For Janet.

Umiatsiaasara pullattagaq nimerussanik ulikkaarpoq.

TORKILK MØRCH

MØRCH (1894-1940), a native of Nuuk (formerly Godthåb), was a pioneer in Greenlandic poetry, combining the archaic rhythms of native culture with the sophistication of cosmopolitan modernism that opened the doors of literature to the generations that followed him. He was educated in Copenhagen, Paris, and Bucharest. His three slender volumes are *Aurora Borealis* (1916), *The Herring Elegies* (1927), and *The Beckoning Foghorns* (1934). Inger Christensen said that Mørch "understood the world and the universe as a continuum of correspondences." He disappeared into a crevasse in 1940, reportedly with a nearly complete book of poems that he carried with him in a small sealskin notebook.

ICE

In the heart of the ice is fire.

You can touch it, feel it,

and sometimes, in the right light

see the blue flame at its heart,

unbearable heat and unbearable cold

married, as the moon and sun are married

together in a love that is much like hatred.

DARKNESS

Summer is torment, a lavishness of light

that beats down relentless into our dazzled eyes

until we yearn for winter's return and the darkness

we had nearly learned to live with. A silent wife

is nonetheless there. Her reliable sulky presence

is a bulwark against one's loneliness and madness.

LIGHT

Unable to sleep, we are always tired. The eye

of day stares down, relentless as a god

inspecting our defects that in these endless days

of exquisitely protracted light are glaring.

Shadows dog our footsteps. In our fatigue

they begin to seem malevolent. The darkness

we hated for so long we begin to long for.

SNOWMEN

The children in America built snowmen,

toys, with funny hats and charcoal eyes,

maybe a pipe, maybe an old scarf.

Ha-ha! The snow would want to keep warm that way!

Greenlandic children may not be any wiser

but they know enough to recognize brute power,

to respect the snow, to honor it and to fear it.

Wallace Stevens glimpsed it at least a little,

not as a child but a sad old man in search

of a metaphor for his marriage, silent, cold,

the nothing that is not there and the nothing that is.

Our children know that both those nothings can bite.

NUNÂ

She is an island, rock rising out of the sea,

gaudy, an old woman with too much make-up,

the white of the guano, the orange-yellow of lichen

smeared on her face in a slap-dash way, suggesting

that she doesn't give a damn what anyone thinks.

But then, why should she? She stands there, an old whore,

waiting for fisherman, the wind and the tide just right,

and the little boats come, like desperate boys. She takes

all comers and gives them the time of their lives.

BEAR, FISHING

In the slow slosh

a quick flash

and the big bear

catches the fish,

putting off for the instant

all that size

to seize,

like a small skittering thing,

the fleeting morsel.

GREENLAND SHARKS

They are slow, they swim very deep, and catch what they can

by ambush more likely than not. The meat of this shark

is poison. Of course it is. But then what desperate

fisherman or his wife decided, despite

what they had learned, or seen with their own eyes

of their neighbors' deaths, that maybe if you boiled it,

not once, but several times, or if you dried it

and ate it then, it wouldn't kill you. It's true:

both methods work, but what grim necessity drove them

to such an experiment as to win this knowledge?

PLANS

A mall! With fountains, palm trees, music of course,

and Chinese food and pizza in the food court.

Shops that feature sun-glasses, running shoes,

greeting cards, tee shirts, and fountain pens.

A tanning salon. Why not? And foot massages.

All the things Nuuk doesn't have.

                                        I see it,

Its dancing neon signs light up the sky

in the winter night and beckon, offering people

the brighter tomorrow Greenlanders deserve.

SLUSH

The ice softens

as the earth comes into her season.

The reindeer revive and the caribou,

the bears in their lairs wake,

and we give thanks to them and for them,

whose helplessness we share.

But only we bear the burden

of knowing our lives are short.

AIR-SPIRIT

I remember the day I first knew you.

I climbed the hills of Sermilik

and from their height gazed out over the wide sea,

and I discovered the vastness

of all that water and, over it, all that air.

The clouds move and the waves move

as the air spirit smoothes or tousles them,

gentle or rough.

                    Be gentle to me,

bring me good luck. Be kind to me,

bring me much seal blubber.

STONE CARVER

The sculptor frees the figure from the stone,

working between what he desires himself

and what the stone allows. The Greenlandic word

"Eqqumiitsuliorneq" means "to create

things that look strange". Or, in other words, "art."

But what can be as strange as the ice formation

the wind chisels and then will obliterate

in its restlessness or its quest for greater strangeness?

It is all the same. The wind's spirit breathes

into the sculptor's mouth, his nose, his hands.

ALCOOLS

The Germans, believe it or don't, claim to have ice wine,

which I'm told they make from the pressing of frozen grapes.

But the name suggests something different and even better,

a hardy vine able to grow on the ice,

where men in anoraks and clumsy gloves

painstakingly harvest its tiny grapes in the snow.

Not for us, but the gods, whose drink it would be.

All those beers and wines and distilled spirits

the continent makes so much of, and so much of,

would be, in comparison, swill. Our rarer cuvée,

the connoisseur's dream, the recovering drunkard's
       nightmare,

might serve to remind them what is important in life.

They might even think how to clean up their lives, to breathe

intoxicatingly cold air at first light.

HOT SPRING

The Danes explain the hot springs as being produced

by tectonic plates grinding against each other

miles below the earth. And it may be so.

No gods. No spirits. No miraculous sign

of any relenting in our ubiquitous coldness.

But they say they know more than us about many things.

Still, when it comes down to it, can you be dumber

than the Dane I saw in the harbor trying to mount

his outboard motor onto his boat's transom.

I had to explain to him that he had it all wrong.

The propeller goes in the water. Not in the boat.

CONCRETE JUNGLE

The fog comes in and the mountains recede and blur

turning into ideas; the promontory

dives into what we presume is water,

and for lack of data's clarity we imagine

whatever we like, escaping to otherness.

To jungles, for instance, or bustling cities, or both,

oddly conflated so that the asphalt streets

are teeming with cougars, impalas, foxes, and wildcats,

snarling at one another. The famous skyscrapers

are all festooned with lianas from which bright birds

make their loud and raucous calls that sound

derisive although they aren't to other birds

but only to us. In the shimmer of heat

the concrete jungle sways and seems to dance…

And the fog lifts, and we find ourselves back in Greenland—

happy, of course, but perhaps not altogether.

MUSIC

A word for music? We never had one

until the Vikings came with the tautirut[*],

The only instruments we ever had were drums,

skins stretched taught and banged with a walrus bone

for dancing to.

                    They thought

we were crude, stupid,

but what is the point of a word except to rule out

everything else, whatever isn't music?

---

[*] A kind of zither similar to the Icelandic Fiðla.

The question I would ask the Europeans

is what isn't music. It's all around us always.

You have to be able to listen. And not to think.

GERDA HVISTERDAHL

Ms. HVISTERDAHL (1916-1994) was born and raised in Qaqortoq. She was an autodidact, a mystic, and a well-known stone carver. Rebelling against Vangardist formulas, she wrote traditional poems about the complexities of man-in-nature. Her *Signs of Habitation* (1952) was awarded the Thule Prize of the Greenlandic Academy of Arts and Letters. *Musk Ox Meat* (1961), which broods about the island's traditional hunter-gatherer culture and the impact upon it of the money economy, was included in the Arctic Cultural Counsel's list of 50 Great Greenlandic books.

THE BLUE WINGED TEAL

They are dabbling ducks, modest birds you would think,

but their range is enormous, from here to the Amazon

and even beyond. And what do they tell those parrots

that rule those roosts and cry to the high heavens

of the grudging north, the bite of our cold air?

Down there, in the heat and rot, the roil of life

is drunk in its plenitude, but its blandishments

to indolence are not in the end persuasive.

One day in the early spring they again decide

that enough is enough and all together take wing

for the strenuous haul north over empty ocean

to return to our bracing marshes and rocky shores.

WHERE

The herds are there somewhere. They have to be.

But they know that I'm coming and run away to hide.

Where can they go? Where could they have gone?

In all this glare and metaphysical whiteness,

how can they not be seen?

                                           But the answer is

that they can see me, a hopeless hungry man

trudging slowly across the landscape. They move

a little further on. If they could, they'd laugh.

FEARS

I fear the weather spirit,

I fear the darkness,

I fear the souls of the animals I have killed,

I fear wicked shamans,

But most of all I fear Takánakapsâluk,

the great woman who lives under the sea,

who rules the sea beasts.

Her gifts to us are grudging and meager.

Her demands are great.

NIVIARSIAQ

The name means "girl" or "maiden"

so you'd think it was shy, hiding out, but no,

like girls, they play, the niviarsissat*,

rollicking purple, taunting the big bluebells

that can also cover a hillside. Like girls their season

is grand but brief, as if the long wait each year

were some dismal school from which, at last, at last,

they are let out at recess when they run riot.

---

* The Greenlandic plural of *niviarsiaq*.

SPEARMEN

They are gone, the old men with spears,

with hoarfrost in their beards, with ice in their lashes,

tracking the reindeer, running like men

after running beasts.

The beasts they chased and killed

are nearly gone,

no match for our lesser men with better weapons.

The old hunters look down and wait

for the spirits to make it fair, to make it right,

and give the reindeer, the caribou, and the musk-ox

guns with which to fight back and in rage and in honor,

thin the herd of men.

LOON

A clear night in winter and the sky

was so cold it was all the stars could do

to hold their places and twinkle to try to keep warm.

One little star, far to the north, in despair

and fear, lost hope, lost light and height, and fell

to the earth where it lay near death. But a loon found it,

and it called to the others with that strange tremolo cry

that startled the stunned star. Then the loons ascended

in the slow clumsiness of their kind that requires much effort

but gets them at last aloft. If the bird could do it,

the star resolved to try again, and succeeded.

And the loons called out, as if it were one of them.

WAKE

A good lover gives way as the water gives way

to the boat's prow, but also, like the water,

cradles, supports, caresses the length of the keel,

and then gives thanks in the celebrating wake

that lets the rest of the sea see what it was.

INSULT POEM

There are sled dogs, hard working but not so bright,

but still brighter than you.

There are also guard dogs, testy, hostile, but useful.

You are like them, except that you are not useful.

And then there are dogs that roam the village for scraps

and seem to be good only for leaving shit

wherever people walk.

    You are just like them.

MUKLUKS

They are not merely boots but the voice of the snow,

eliciting now a steady rhythmic scrunch,

and now a whisper, and now, on the frozen surface,

a sibilant sound. Gulls have their cries for danger,

for hunger, for calling mates. But the snow doesn't care

and sings to itself however it feels that moment,

or rather it waits for one of us in mukluks

for the chance to express whatever it may be feeling.

DEATH DOG

He's a tracking dog, and he trails me, snuffles along

and picks up my scent on the ice. Sometimes I hear him

getting nearer and nearer. I hurry away

but now and then turn, stand my ground, and shout:

"Keep away, death dog. Keep away from me. Any closer,

and I'll hitch you to my sled and put you to work."

INNUNQUAQ LARSEN

LARSEN (1935-2002) was born in Qeqertarsuatsiaat on the southwestern coast. His long narrative poem about the seeress Þorkell is widely studied in Greenlandic secondary schools and esteemed among literary critics for its keen understanding of the pagan culture and the celebration of objects that were a part of the island's spiritual history. He was fluent both in Greenlandic and Danish, but his poetry was entirely in Greenlandic. Aside from his *Þorkell's Knife* (1960) his work appeared in a series of eleven *Fascicles* that were published in letter-press pamphlet form from 1971 until the onset of his deep depression in 1978, during which he was hospitalized and from which he never recovered.

STONE KNIFE

The stone had been waiting for thousands of years

with a patience we cannot imagine

for the hand that would come among them all,

each of them dreaming "choose me, choose me,"

and this was the chosen.

The blows against the other stones were painful,

but the stone blade would remember and wreak that pain

on soft flesh like that of the hand that held it,

taking as much satisfaction as the man did,

doing his bidding,

as it never minded, for stone can outlive any man.

And lie there again, wherever he might have dropped it,

waiting, as it knew how to do for the other

hand that could come to pick it up, for the eye

that would know what it was, for the mind, soft but sharp

enough to greet it and pay it proper reverence.

HELL

The missionaries came and preached to us

about the fires of hell. Hey, not so bad!

All that wood to keep the fires going

all day and all night? I could stand that.

It isn't frightening anyway. Polite,

we didn't giggle. We even hid our smiles.

We know that if there's a hell it is either cold there

or else it always swarms with savage mosquitoes.

HALLUCINATIONS

The death by water is quick,

and the death by freezing is slow.

But the death by hunger,

an exquisite dwindling,

offers some of its victims the gift

of visions of beasts we have never encountered,

of tall trees with ripe fruits,

of women, dancing and singing,

or simply of food, musk-ox or harp-seal meat,

and beautiful chewy blubber, all they could want

and more. Ja-jija. Ja-jija.

SENSES

The five we agree on, but what of the other subtle

information systems the brain relies on?

Balance is surely a sense. And kinesthetics,

the knowledge of where the parts of the body are

and how much an object weighs upon the muscles

that lift it to learn how heavy it is. Distension

is also a sense, the need to shit or pee

or fart. At the other end, the vagus nerve

announces nausea, doesn't merely report

but predicts, which is what our senses are for. And fear?

Is that an emotion? Or, when our hair stands up,

a part of the sensorium? Sleepiness?

Vertigo? The meat and bone rely

on the nerves' news for survival, and we should acknowledge

how, on a certain street, in a certain room,

where it doesn't feel right, something dismal impends,

and if we are smart we'll try to get away.

BEGGING FOR SEAL OIL

I lie on this bench, sick, useless,

and cannot even fetch seal oil for the lamp.

My wife goes begging. "Borrowing," she calls it,

but they're not stupid and know we can never repay them.

Reindeer skin for our clothes, meat for our meals,

she "borrows" all this

                           while I lie here on this bench,

my face turned to the wall, waiting to die.

RETURN

To hunt the bear, you have to become the bear,

not think as a man but react as a bear would react.

To hunt the caribou you must for the while

become the caribou. And the reindeer herd,

and the walrus and the seal. The hunter's spirit

yields to the animal's spirit. It's only fair.

It takes young men a long time to learn this skill,

but after a time, they get it, some more, some less.

What's harder and takes much longer to learn is how

to come back after the hunt to rejoin the village

and become a man again, ascending or else

descending to be what he was and what we are.

FOUR QUESTIONS

I have grown old and learned much,

but there are four things I do not know

and have despaired of learning.

Ha ya yo.

Where did the sun come from?

How does the moon change in the sky?

How do the minds of women work?

And why do so many people have lice?

Ha ya yo.

DANCING

Mostly life is hard,

hunger the spear in us

that drives our spears into the caribou

if we can find them.

But sometimes, with a full belly,

around the fire, we see each other

in the dancing light.

We are like the weeds on a rock in the river,

swaying in the current,

happy, dancing.

GOING INTO THE INTERIOR

When a man is sick and knows he cannot recover,

or shamed so that he cannot recover from that,

betrayed by his wife-swap friend,

or too old to run after the reindeer,

he travels away from the coast toward the looming
      mountains,

the highest mountain, Gunnbjørn, with ice and sheer stone,

to die of course but also perhaps to become

transformed into a powerful spirit, a ghost

that can come back down to the coast and live forever,

helping those few who showed him kindnesses

and following those who hurt him or were indifferent

with powerful curses that bring unending back luck.

ARGUMENT FOR THE DEFENSE

They are saying that Padloq killed the cripple

and stole his caribou meat.

                              I don't believe it.

Not because he is above suspicion, oh, no!

But Padloq is a lazy tub of guts,

an eater of carcasses and also a coward.

Such a deed would have been beyond his powers.

CROWDS

How fine to see the reindeer

trotting together in the early spring.

It is fine to see the musk-oxen huddled together

for protection against the hunters' dogs.

It is fine to see the girls coming out of school,

giggling like so many twittering starlings.

It is fine to see the crowd of boys staring

at them torn between shyness and desire.

DEPARTURES

The eyes go that used to follow the game,

and the legs that used to take him for miles and miles,

and the arm that pulled the bowstring back to the ear

or paddled the kayak against the outgoing tide.

The dick goes too, goes limp. And at last the mind,

unable to bear any more, speaks to the man:

"Go out to sea, farther than you can return from.

The sea mother waits in her underwater palace

to give you whatever welcome you may deserve."

WHY THE ARCTIC HARE HAS SHORT EARS

When Þorkell, the great shaman tripped and fell,

he hit his head on a rock.

He was knocked cold,

but still his *anak·ua** was bright enough

to summon a passing hare.

He could have frozen to death if the hare had not

appeared and seen him, and sat upon his chest

sharing with him its little body's heat.

When Þorkell awoke, he thanked the brave hare and offered

whatever gift the animal might choose.

---

* Greenlandic for "shamanic glow".

"My ears are too long," the hare said. "They get cold.

Could you make them shorter?" And Þorkell laughed aloud

and granted him that boon. And offered another.

"Such a modest request, such a modest gift.

You deserve more than that. What else would you like?"

The hare said that, being only a hare,

he had no idea what to ask for. "You decide."

And Þorkell said, "Your sense of smell is keen,

but I will make it keener. Now you can find

sweet twigs under the snow." He patted the hare,

thanked him once again, and wished him well.

GLACIER

It isn't the crack of the ice that brings on fear,

for I have survived that moment: it didn't kill me.

But when will the next come, when will the ice

give way to whatever pressures have been building?

The silence is different now from what it was

before that sound. It is fearsome, and now the feet

turn tentative, each step along the way

the one that may be the last. And then the next.

My spirit wants me to stop, stand still. But I tell it

that I would freeze to death, and that fear goads me

to keep on walking, balanced between two terrors.

DIALOGUE OF THE SISTERS

1st Sister:

I am hungry, hungry.

If I were a bear, I could tear

beasts into meat

to bite with my teeth.

2nd Sister:

If I were a wolf, I could bite with my fangs.

1st Sister:

Or a caribou. I could strike with my antlers.

2nd Sister:

Or a walrus, with my tusks.

1st Sister:

Or the loud thunder, with my

tongue of forked lightning.

THE ORPHAN

His mother died in childbirth.

His father took to drink then, and disappeared,

inland, or out to sea. He was left alone

to shift for himself, to beg for scraps, to endure

however he could the harshness of a village

that a difficult life makes hard. His schoolmates mocked him

for his raggedy clothes, his habit of looking away

when anyone spoke to him, his answering stammer.

Not the childhood or youth anyone would want,

but all that yearning for love and hatred of meanness

combined in him, transformed his battered heart

to make him the shaman he has become. We fear him,

but we respect him, and understand we deserve him.

BREATH

You can see them in winter,

each breath making a cloud as it hits the cold

so that it is visible, seems alive,

and you watch a poem form and disappear,

or is it a prayer?

In the summer you also breathe.

You cannot see your breath,

but you know it is there,

can remember what it looked like

enough to believe.

GAME OF THE GODS

All the time worrying about this prayer and that,

this desperate fisherman, that luckless hunter,

the gods sometimes need some relaxation,

and they play soccer up in the sky's field,

kicking a walrus skull and running and laughing.

Those are the northern lights that shimmer and play,

the shadows of their spirits as they move.

My baby was born last night while the lights were playing.

A good omen: he will be smart and strong.

MICE

No doubt, the Danes brought them, hidden away

in the cargo somewhere and we have them now in plenty,

food for the cats, dogs, owls, foxes and weasels,

but pets, sometimes, for the children who feel sorry

for the tiny, filthy, helpless things. In a cage

they survive but never for long. They starve to death,

or the cat will manage to get them.

Their deaths are instructive—

what children need in order to grow up a little

and begin to know themselves and all of us

who are also tiny, filthy, helpless things.

LOVE POEMS

There haven't been any here. Everywhere else

they write love poems, sing love songs, complain

that love is not always easy, or celebrate

how good it can be. Not here. We know these things

too well to have to say them. Coming back from a hunt

at sea or in the fjords, or out on the ice,

what can anyone say about human warmth

and the way feeling comes back to the hands and feet?

These are occasions rather for prayers of thanksgiving.

ROADS

The cities have them, and even some of the towns,

but they all go only so far and then give out,

sometimes to a track that also gives out, and then...

you are there; you are back on the land or the ice, as naked,

as wild as it ever was. A huge beast

one would think was trapped, it can, whenever it wants,

shrug, stretch, set itself free again.

You do not need to be a shaman to know this.

Just go to the end of the road and then look ahead.

LULLABY

Sleep, little one, dreaming pacific dreams

I cannot even imagine. What can you want?

Warm all the time, fed whenever you cry,

you dream of waking life, which is a dream.

The dreams of milk will soon enough change to meat,

and to nightmares of cold and hunger. But never mind.

You cannot imagine the meaning of my words.

So sleep, wrapped warm in your sealskin in my arms.

TEARS

tears

freeze

the cheek

sears

along the streak

but then in some

brief time

goes numb

HISTORY

Who else has such a history? People came,

desperate they must have been, or driven by madness,

and lived here and died out. The Saqqaqs came,

declined, and disappeared, And the next and the next.

But the truth reasserted itself, and there were gaps,

centuries long, when no one was here. And the island

queened it with only the bears and the caribou

and the birds calling out their proud and derisive cries.

A Greenlander has to acknowledge this and admit

modestly that we are temporary.

But then, in those proud empires far to the south,

they are guests too, no different from us.

ABOUT THE TRANSLATORS

Nive Grønkjær is professor of Inuit Studies at the University of Baffin Island and director of the Knut Rasmussen Kalaalit Nunaat Institute.

David R. Slavitt is an established translator of Greek, Latin, Hebrew, Italian, Portuguese, and Sanskrit.

CPSIA information can be obtained
at www.ICGtesting.com
Printed in the USA
BVHW082340161221
624066BV00004B/262

9 780984 943937